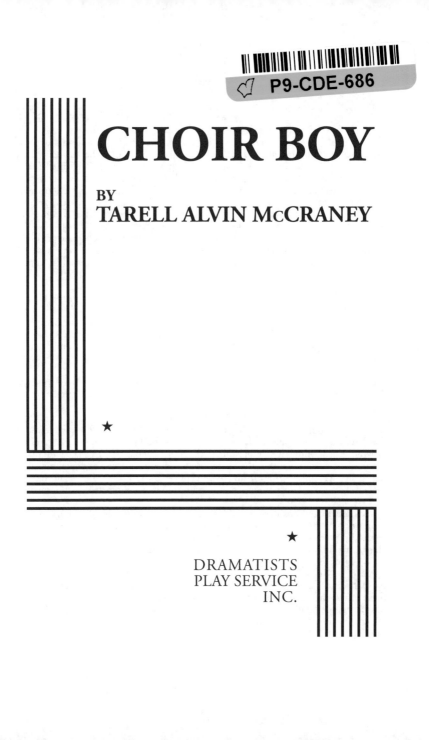

CHOIR BOY

BY
TARELL ALVIN McCRANEY

★

DRAMATISTS
PLAY SERVICE
INC.

CHOIR BOY
Copyright © 2014, Tarell Alvin McCraney

All Rights Reserved

2

For Saleem

CHOIR BOY was presented by Manhattan Theatre Club (Lynne Meadow, Artistic Director; Barry Grove, Executive Producer) in a co-production with Alliance Theater (Susan V. Booth, Artistic Director), at City Center Stage II in New York City, opening on July 2, 2013. It was directed by Trip Cullman; the set and costume designs were by David Zinn; the lighting design was by Peter Kaczorowski; the sound design was by Fitz Patton; the music direction and vocal arrangements were by Jason Michael Webb; and the production stage manager was Kyle Gates. The cast was as follows:

HEADMASTER MARROW..................................Chuck Cooper
PHARUS JONATHAN YOUNG .... Jeremy Pope
MR. PENDLETON ....Austin Pendleton
BOBBY MARROW... Wallace Smith
JUNIOR DAVIS.. Nicholas L. Ashe
ANTHONY JUSTIN "AJ" JAMES .... Grantham Coleman
DAVID HEARD .... Kyle Beltran

CHARACTERS

HEADMASTER MARROW — Late 30s/early 40s man of color, is the youngest and latest headmaster for the Charles R. Drew Prep School for Boys. He is paternal uncle to Bobby Marrow.

PHARUS JONATHAN YOUNG — Late teens, an effeminate young man of color. Begins the play a junior at the Charles R. Drew Prep School for Boys and the lead of the school's famous choir. He is roommates with AJ James.

MR. PENDLETON — Late 60s/70s, white male, professor at the Charles R. Drew Prep School for Boys.

BOBBY MARROW — Mid- to late teens, a young man of color, Bobby is a junior at the Charles R. Drew Prep School and a member of the school's choir. He is also nephew to Headmaster Marrow.

JUNIOR DAVIS — A teenage young man of color, and a junior at the Charles R. Drew Prep School for Boys. He is a member of the school's choir.

ANTHONY JUSTIN "AJ" JAMES — Late teens, an athletic young man of color, a senior at the Charles R. Drew Prep School for Boys. He is a member of the school's choir and the school's baseball team. He is roommates with Pharus Young.

DAVID HEARD — Late teens, a young man of color, a senior at the Charles R. Drew Prep School for Boys. He is a member of the school's choir.

PLACE

Charles R. Drew Prep School for Boys.

TIME

A school year, last year.

CHOIR BOY

PROLOGUE/GRADUATION

The stage is bare save for a few chairs. A spotlight warms on Headmaster Marrow.

HEADMASTER. Ladies and gentlemen, family and friends,
Welcome to the 49th Commencement for the
Charles R. Drew Prep School for Boys.
And now to present the school song, next year's Choir Lead. Mr.
Pharus Jonathan Young.
(Pharus steps forward and sings "Trust and Obey," the school's song. With this the commencement begins.)
PHARUS.
  When we walk with the Lord
  in the light of His Word,
  what a glory He sheds on our way!
  While we do His good will,
  he abides with us still,
  and with all who will trust and obey.
  Trust and obey, for there's no other way
  to be happy in Jesus, but to trust and —
(Pharus has stopped. The headmaster notices. Pharus looks behind him and is about to continue when we shift.)

AN OFFICE

HEADMASTER. *(Taking off his robe.)* I said it, I reminded you at rehearsal in April, didn't I?

PHARUS. Yes, Headmaster Marrow.

HEADMASTER. I said, "Pharus, whatever you do, don't stop singing the school Song until every student is gathered and seated on that stage."
What'd you say then?

HEADMASTER and PHARUS. Why?

HEADMASTER. I knew right then
Right then, you would take that opportunity to
Be defiant, trouble ...

PHARUS. Trouble, sir?

HEADMASTER. Up to something!
I'm up there explaining to the board why ...
You think I want to be explaining anything to the board?
"Why *him*?" they asked. "Why *that* one?"
"Well he's the best, regardless of his ... "

PHARUS. You said that about me sir?

HEADMASTER. Yes —

PHARUS. I mean, it's true, but you said?

HEADMASTER. Pharus!

PHARUS. Sir?

HEADMASTER. Why, after I asked you not to, told you, "you couldn't,"
Made you understand the tradition, pointed out its
Potency, did you get up there at the Seniors' graduation,
A day that should afford them every rite and ritual
Of the ceremony, and mess up their moment
Why?

PHARUS. I ... Would you rather be feared or respected, Headmaster?

HEADMASTER. Pharus!

PHARUS. It keeps me up at night.

HEADMASTER. It does not.

PHARUS. *(Moving ahead.)* Now see,
If you're respected people give you space

But if they fear you, they jumpin' back off of curbs ...
HEADMASTER. Son, what does this have to do with you breaking
a 49-year-old Tradition?
What does this have to do with me needing to get
Your mama on the phone because the board wants you expelled?
Or to take away your scholarship which they know means you can't
Attend.
PHARUS. I can't afford to ...
HEADMASTER. Few of you could!
But there you have it, a financial crisis, two years on this job, and I
got board members
Talking about withdrawing money! All because ...
PHARUS. Sir you can't ... I earned that scholarship.
HEADMASTER. I know.
PHARUS. And that place in singing the song, sir, you said ...
HEADMASTER. I did.
PHARUS. Don't let them!
HEADMASTER. You are tying my hands. Give me some answers.
I could say ... Did you get nervous?
PHARUS. I am a professional.
HEADMASTER. Something caught in your throat?
PHARUS. *(Referring to his throat.)* This the Lord's passageway, let
no follicle formed against me prosper.
HEADMASTER. Pharus!
PHARUS. I got ... did ... was distracted.
HEADMASTER. By what!
PHARUS. All of the pomp and circumstance and all,
So much noise and ...
I was overwhelmed and in "awe" of my dear school
Thinking soon and very soon this, those graduating, that will be me.
HEADMASTER. Why were you turned around?
PHARUS. There was something swelling at the back.
HEADMASTER. Don't lie.
PHARUS. Sir!
There is nothing I want to do more than be
And act as a Drew man should.
I try to conduct my behavior by the book.
I do not lie.

And I don't snitch.

HEADMASTER. What? Huh. So …
So someone … distracted you?

Someone was talking to you onstage?
PHARUS. *To* me?
HEADMASTER. About you … Calling you …
PHARUS. Everything but a child of God. And I'm sorry, sir,
I … Jumped, sir, but luckily not too far. I heard
That whisper and I didn't answer back I just
Kept on singing. And everything worked out alright,
Right? In the end it was all of four, five seconds?
HEADMASTER. Huh. I'm … Huh. I see.
I'm sorry. I lost my temper.
Listen …
PHARUS. I was voted next year's choir lead, almost unanimously,
you hear?
HEADMASTER. That's quite an honor, a privilege …
At least, it was in my day.
PHARUS. I know, I'm ready, I want you to be proud too, sir.
HEADMASTER. That Choir means a lot to this school. We've
relied on its Support since …
PHARUS. *(By rote.)* Founded by the second headmaster who heard
A group of boys singing in the showers, and decided
To use a choir to gain attention and financial support
For the Little All-Boys School That Could. Why the Headmaster
was close enough to hear them boys singing in the
Showers I'll never know.
HEADMASTER. Pharus …
PHARUS. But that was olden times,
People was just more closer then, I guess.
HEADMASTER. Pharus …
PHARUS. Sir? *(Pharus' wrist goes limp.)*
HEADMASTER. *(He looks and corrects Pharus' limp wrist.)* I need
to speak to the student who was calling you …
Things on the choir stand.
PHARUS. I can't say.
HEADMASTER. I … right. I know you don't want to be a stool
pigeon …
PHARUS. Ha! Oh Headmaster you're so Colombo; "stool pigeon"?
HEADMASTER. Who was it, Pharus!

PHARUS. You know the rule
A Drew man doesn't tell on his brother,
PHARUS and HEADMASTER. "He allows him the honor to confess himself."
PHARUS. It may seem silly but ever since I was a little boy
I've wanted to grow up and be a Drew man. I couldn't
Possibly say who *they* were.
HEADMASTER. They?
PHARUS. Have a good summer, Headmaster. *(Shift.)*

A HALL

BOBBY. The first day …
JUNIOR. Bobby.
BOBBY. First day of class!
JUNIOR. Yo!
BOBBY. And this Nigga!
JUNIOR. Don't you get tired of that word?
BOBBY. Nigga see a nigga, gone call him nigga.
Ain't even get to school good, didn't even
Get a chance to know my schedule, this …
Damn!
JUNIOR. It's over now. It's Choir now.
BOBBY. What I look like, a slave? Got me out there
Booker T. Washingtonin' that quad man, like I'm …
He supposed to get them scholarship boys for that.
JUNIOR. I'm on scholarship.
BOBBY. Partial, Junior, 'on't be admitting that. Shit,
My people ain't paying so I learn no …
I wish my daddy could find out!
JUNIOR. You gone tell him?
BOBBY. Stch, He too busy with Rita!
JUNIOR. How is your step-mom?
BOBBY. *(Shrugs.)* Step-mom.
Stch, Damn! Trash duty on the first day of school.
And for what?
JUNIOR. I mean, he is your uncle.

11

BOBBY. When we here he Headmaster Marrow.
JUNIOR. Bobby calm down. What's left? We done now,
We at rehearsal.
BOBBY. I know he snitched.
JUNIOR. Who, Pharus? Don't nobody snitch at Drew.
BOBBY. Don't nobody suppose to swish at Drew neither
But we two for two.
Wait 'til I see him. Wait 'til he walk in.
Nigga gone get it. Pause.
JUNIOR. How you know it was Pharus?
BOBBY. Who else it gone be? Uncle Steve gone call
Me in his office talking 'bout, "You know I ain't
Forgot about what happened at commencement last."
I'm like, "huh?" He go, "If you can 'huh' you can hear
You on trash duty." I'm like "what for?"
He talking about some, "play dumb but play dumb
Out on that quad while you getting that rubbish, Bobby,
And take Junior with you." Ooh!
I started to go bust Pharus up right then. You just wait …
JUNIOR. Just leave 'em alone.
BOBBY. What you sweet on him? Don't tell me I gotta watch
My cheeks 'round you too.
JUNIOR. Bobby don't … *(Pharus, David, and AJ enter.)*
PHARUS. Welcome back, Welcome back everybody.
This is the day the Lord hath made …
C'mon on y'all rejoice and be glad!
Take these, sit, arrange yourselves in order of
Tenor Baritone Bass. The first rehearsal
Of the Charles Drew Chorus is about to begin,
(Bobby walks up on Pharus.) Bobby?
JUNIOR. C'mon man. How you doin', Pharus?
PHARUS. Blessed and Highly favored how you, Junior?
Y'all alright? Who came to make a joyful *noice*!
AJ. Why you so happy?
PHARUS. Leading Anthony Justin takes volume and front foot.
Now, I'm sure y'all are excited to be back. And didn't
Expect to be meeting so soon. With Ms. Jamison on leave
Just Pregnant, we are without a sponsor so
Until the Headmaster appoints someone to take her place
I figured we could learn music and get ready …

DAVID. For?

PHARUS. "For?"

For!

This is the year I lead the Charles Drew Prep Choir

And its 50th anniversary. We have to be on point

And though just the fall, Spring Gala is a-coming, fast.

I need to whip these voices into a blend so beautiful

They gone rename the Choir: "Seraphim," Yes Father!

I've already done some new arrangements on the more traditional …

BOBBY. Who asked you to do that?

PHARUS. It's my prerogative as Choir lead.

JUNIOR. Pre — what?

DAVID. His right.

BOBBY. Eh, don't be pushing dem kinda rights up in here.

AJ. Bobby, what are you talking about?

PHARUS. Don't worry fellas, I'm new at this but not to music.

This I know. And I just thought the traditional Spiritual

Could use a li'l melody more modern but we still …

BOBBY. Stch.

PHARUS. You singing with us today or you got something else in your Mouth.

BOBBY. You trying to be funny?

JUNIOR. Uh, no he trying to tell you to take the gum out.

BOBBY. It's my prerogative.

JUNIOR. C'mon!

DAVID. You know the rules Bobby, man. *(Pharus blows the pitch pipe.)*

PHARUS. No gum during choir.

BOBBY. You don't run me!

PHARUS. But I do run this choir

I couldn't say a thing last spring when you were calling me out my

Name stood up there before God and country.

BOBBY. But you ran and told the Headmaster faster than your little heels could click.

DAVID. Told?

What's he talking about?

BOBBY. C'mon Pharus tell 'em what I'm talking 'bout.

PHARUS. While serving my duty as tenor in the choir

Singing the school song for the class-just-gone's commencement

Brother Bobby and his homie Junior decided they were going to cuss

Me like street trash.

BOBBY. That's a lie, nigga.
JUNIOR. Bobby, don't do this man.
PHARUS. I ain't gone be too many more lies Bobby Marrow
BOBBY. Junior ain't say nothing
PHARUS. Oh that's right he just snickered. Meanwhile your
Uncle the Good Headmaster calls me into his office mad
'Cause I stopped to look at you fools and nearly kicked me out
The school.
BOBBY. Ha! And that's when you told him, Bobby was talking.
PHARUS. Bobby you do know what you are saying, right?
You saying that I broke a sacred rule that we all
Live by ... If you tell
On one ...
DAVID, AJ, and JUNIOR. You'll tell on all.
PHARUS. And I need my brothers to trust me.
Sure: there are things I could talk about,
Things I could tell about you heading over to
The Public school at night to see that ol' gal
Or how Junior can't but barely read got somebody
Doing his work for him.
JUNIOR. Damn.
PHARUS. There are visions and things that've romp'd these halls
Really would make the Headmaster swing my way but
Contrary to popular belief I ain't into that. So however Mr. Marrow
Found out that nephew Bobby was cutting the fool
On the choir stand it was not from Pharus. I had other things
On my mind.
BOBBY. I bet ...
PHARUS. Like expelling two young ones out of this year's choir.

I was going t' let you know that because of your
Attitude and the consensus of the choir that
You can make things uncomfortable you were
On probation but since you came in here, First Day, and,
Forgive me lord, showed your natural black ass
I think we can forgo probation and move to put
You out.
BOBBY. You can't do that.
PHARUS. Aw Bobby what you were saying about me on the
Stand, you, of all people shouldn't be surprised at

14

What I can do. And do well.
Now if you and your friend will excuse us we got
An anniversary to ready for
David, did you want to lead us in the prayer?
(Bobby exits. David and AJ kneel.)
Junior I'm sorry boy I was being unfair you
Didn't say anything. You are more than welcome
To stay. And I am sorry I lumped you in like
That. I should be ashamed. I of all people know
What it feels like to be accused 'cause of association.
Huh, we could lose our best …
What you sing again?
JUNIOR. *(Proud.)* Baritone now. Can't you hear?
PHARUS. Ooh voice just growing up! Low huh?
Let's pray. Try to Blend …
For the Lord at least.
(Pharus looks to Junior, smiles, and goes to pray.)
DAVID.

> *O ah couldn't hear nobody pray*
>> BOYS.
>>> *Lord, A-couldn't hear nobody pray*
>>> *O way down yonder by myself*
>>> *And ah couldn't hear nobody pray*

> *In the valley*

>>> *A-couldn't hear nobody pray*

> *On my knees*

>>> *A-couldn't hear nobody pray*

JUNIOR.
> *With my burden*

>>> *Way down yonder by myself*

DAVID.
> *Cryin' "Savior!"*

>> ALL.
>>> *A-couldn't hear nobody pray*

Chilly waters

    A-couldn't hear nobody pray

In the Jordan

    A-couldn't hear nobody pray

Crossing over
(Shift.)

SOLUS

HEADMASTER. … deciding to leave the cages open in the science lab,
And tagging the doors with Underground Rail Road,
is not funny nor is it the best way to dissent dissection. You may think of yourselves as some sort of PETA/animal rights Harriet Tubman but
let me be clear: you are vandalizing school property. Which will not be tolerated.
Let Us be honorable Drew Men, those responsible should
Come forward now, report to me your stance against dissection and there may be less Punishment but some repayment Program put in place. To everyone else:
A great first week to kick off our 50th year Anniversary, all schedules kept,
All rooms clean. Keep your minds Clear, and your hands in prayer. Five minutes and lights out.

A ROOM

AJ. You trying to be the only tenor left standing!
I'm mean that's what it look like, that's what everyone gone think.
PHARUS. I gave up on thinking for everybody a semester ago.
It's hard but you should try …
AJ. Tell the truth
PHARUS. And shame the devil. Hey we haven't EVEN talked about summers yet
How was yours, Roomie? You bag you a honey Or whatever you homies in Willacoochie, call it? Hurry tell me we got five until …
AJ. I ain't forgot …
PHARUS. Huh?
AJ. Sophomore year,
You in this room by yourself, they
Move me in 'cause nobody would room with yah.
PHARUS. Are you unhappy here?
You can change rooms any time you would
Like, Anthony Justin James,
AJ. LORD! The full name?!
PHARUS. No one is making you be here.
AJ. I was sleeping right here and I heard you …
PHARUS. How you sleeping and you heard me?
AJ. … Tell your Mama on the phone.
"Mama I'ma be
The first Drew Boy in history to sing a commencement twice!"
PHARUS. That is not what I sound like …
I would never call myself a "Drew boy."
AJ. "I'm the best they got they have to let me sing Junior
Year. Then Senior year …
I will just make it so I can." Sneaky ass!
PHARUS. Lower your voice boy; quiet hours.
AJ. This me you talking to …
You want me to call your Mama?
PHARUS. Lord no. She'll think something wrong
Boy sit your lanky self down just all these
Limbs. Okay, okay … I'm trying to sing the school

17

Song at our Graduation. And not calm like I did
It this past time, I would go glory! Like only I can.
No offense.
AJ. Oh none taken, Pharus man, we all know you got a gift.
PHARUS. Let Him use me.
AJ. But you can't be kicking Bobby
Out to make sure …
PHARUS. Who? The devil is a liar! I did not kick
That mean boy out the choir 'cause he could
Sing … better than me … Oh God I nearly fainted.
I asked him to leave because he is disruptive.
You heard Bobby call me out my name.
AJ. Huh. David called you worse last year …
PHARUS. Yeah, but he apologized
And you just got it in for David.
AJ. I just don't believe his conversion is One Hundred
He 'round here talking 'bout he going to seminary
School.
PHARUS. The Lord works in mysterious ways.
AJ. But the devil has a tireless mind. Don't make
No foe with Bobby Marrow, man,
PHARUS. You know what that son of blessed assurance
Said while I was up there singing?
AJ. Hm.
PHARUS. I'm up there in front of his pappy and all
His relatives who support the school staring forward
And I hear him just giggling
You can't miss Bobby Marrow giggling.
Sound like two fat ladies
Amused by cake, just him. So I just
Sing on and every now I hear him say
BOBBY. Sissy. Dis Sissy
Dis Faggot ass Nigga.
PHARUS. Huh.
Even the custodian, done called
Me out my name, that don't make it right,
But now, in the middle of commencement, really?
I started to turn around but I didn't say anything.
AJ. Why?
PHARUS. It's too much. That would have

18

Brought more attention to call him out like that. Who would
They have believed? The nephew of the School's Headmaster
Or the lil Sweet Boy they been trying to straighten out for years?
I worked hard to get where I am now in this school.
AJ. You been doing Good, man.
PHARUS. Good? I been doing great, it only seem good
Because everybody always want me to do bad.
All the great I got get diminished. Huh, If I was you ...
AJ. You can't be me!
PHARUS. On the baseball team ...
AJ. Can't swing like me.
PHARUS. With that body ...
AJ. Can't ... what?
PHARUS. And *my* grades. I would be the all the rave: But ooh if
they let me sang ...
As it stands, with Bobby gone, they'll look to Junior for commence-
ment of our Class but his voice is too low now so then they'll have
to look to the
Seniors and since they are looking they might as well see ...
AJ. C'mon, don't get stupid, now
PHARUS. Between roomies, I love Drew ...
AJ. I do too.
PHARUS. I will be so sad to go.
AJ. Me too.
PHARUS. But not that dawg on sad.

Paul and Silas, bound to jail	BOYS.
Had no money for to go their bail,	*Ooooh*
	PHARUS and BOYS.
	Keep your eyes on the prize
	Hold on, Hold On
	BOYS.
	Hold on
Hold on	
	Hold on
Hold on	PHARUS and BOYS.
	Keep your eyes on the prize
	Hold on
	BOYS.
	Hold on
Paul and Silas begin to shout,	*Ooooh*

jail door open and they walked out

Ooooh

PHARUS and BOYS.
Keep your eyes on the prize
Hold on, Hold On
BOYS.
Hold on

Hold on

Hold on

Hold on
PHARUS and BOYS.
Keep your eyes on the prize
Hold on, Hold On
BOYS.
Hold on

Hold on

Hold on

Hold on
PHARUS and BOYS.
Keep your eyes on the prize
Hold on

A HALL

HEADMASTER. Understand me, huh! You are to be an example.
This man is coming out of semi-retirement and,
God bless him, would like to engage you all, prep
You for college-life and study. See that you create essays
Worthy of early acceptance. With the board's financial review
Coming up we need you to grade
Up your tests in the spring;
A recommendation from him is no small thing.
It could be your way in or out of higher education.
BOBBY. And a cushy profile for the board.
HEADMASTER. Bobby!
AJ. Headmaster, we already got a lot of classes.
HEADMASTER. What's one more?

20

AJ. One more.

HEADMASTER. What?

BOBBY. Man, I ain't plan on ...

HEADMASTER. I don't even understand why you all are talking! You're already scheduled! *(All groan, save Pharus.)* Right after lunch.

BOBBY. That's my free period!

HEADMASTER. This is school you don't need a free period.

DAVID. I thought it was an elective course, can we ask
Him to teach religion?

HEADMASTER. You don't ask anything. Whatever he says *he's*
Doing, *you're* doing. It's ... a gift to the school on
Its anniversary. What you need to say is, "Thank you
Headmaster."

ALL. Thank you, sir.

HEADMASTER. And afterwards write a nice note to the board.
Now, as soon as he comes I want
You to welcome him and treat him with the utmost
Respect and ...
Dr. Pendleton.

MR. PENDLETON. I'm sorry, so sorry, hello, hello, no doctor
Just Mr. or Pendleton or Mr. P or ... Sorry I'm
See it's not just black people who
Are late.
I mean ... You know with the CPT. See that was a ...
A ... joke. Fellas about the colored peoples ...
Time. Don't leave me out here too long.

I'm Mr. Pendleton. I taught here, well, forever ago.
But I've decided to come
Back and well lead a course in thinking ...

AJ. Ugh.

HEADMASTER. Ey!

MR. PENDLETON. Well no it's not just a course it's a creative thinking course,
When it comes to liberal arts, history, it is an elective
Course so you know, you can *not* take it ...

HEADMASTER. It's required.

MR. PENDLETON. It's required.
And well ...

HEADMASTER. They need a course like this ...

BOBBY. Hm, Taught by a famous historian.
HEADMASTER. Bobby!
MR. PENDLETON. Listen, fellas, can I call you …
HEADMASTER. Students.
MR. PENDLETON. Students,
It's a class that is going to help you think outside
The box. Or try to …
It'll be a fun class.
AJ. Doesn't sound fun.
MR. PENDLETON. It's a course that is about you thinking
About things creatively, if you will …
PHARUS. Critically.
MR. PENDLETON. Yes.
PHARUS. Not just what you teach but how we react to it.
How it engages us and our unique way of understanding
It?
MR. PENDLETON. Very … what's your name?
HEADMASTER and PHARUS. Pharus, sir.
MR. PENDLETON. Good. Good. I don't believe in education …
I mean not in the way … not in the way most do. I believe that there
is information I can give you and that really you teach each other
ways, new ways, to take that information in.
Well listen your first assignment is to give
A theory, a well-known theory, and challenge it.
AJ. Like … like "Relativity"?
MR. PENDLETON. Yes, like the theory of relativity, if you
understand it.
AJ. Good, cuz I don't.
MR. PENDLETON. Neither do I.
Great, see you next class. *(Shift.)*

CALL HOME

The Boys All Call Home.

JUNIOR.
> *I hear*
> *Rockin' in the Land*

> > BOYS.
> > *Rocking in the land,*
> > *And ringing them bells*
> > *I hear, Rockin' in the Land,*
> > *Rocking in the land,*
> > *And ringing them bells*

Hello?
DAVID. Can I place a collect call please?
PHARUS. Hello Mama, Yes Ma'am.
BOBBY. Yes sir, I'm behaving.
AJ. Things going alright, yeah … Ma you got a cold
Or something your voice sounds …
Man, Charlie get off the phone.
Let me speak to mama!

> > *I know oh my Lord there's*
> > *rockin' in the land*
> > *rocking in the land*
> > *And ringing them bells*
> > *I know oh my Lord there's*
> > *rockin' in the land*
> > *rocking in the land*
> > *And ringing them bells*
> > *Rockin' Jerusalem*
> > *Rockin' Jerusalem*
> > *In Jerusalem,*
> > *Ringing them Bells.*

(Hums.)
DAVID. Yeah I tried calling earlier
But nobody would accept the charges. I know it's

23

Expensive, sir, I just wanted to see how y'all were doing.
I know … I know … Dad!
I'm doing alright. Sorry to … Yes sir. I … Yeah I know
They are expensive calls. I hear you, sir. And I'm … well
That's what I wanted to … I'm trying to tell you. One of my grades
slipped.
I know you can't and I'm trying to hold on but this new class …
JUNIOR. Hello?
> *Church getting high*
> *Church getting Higher Jerusalem*
> *Ring them Bells*
> *Church getting high*
> *Church getting Higher Jerusalem*
> *Ring them Bells My Lord,*

PHARUS. Yes Ma'am
BOBBY. Night sir.
AJ. I love you too Ma.
Drop dead Charlie.
JUNIOR. Hell … Stch.
DAVID. I will. Yes sir. Good night.
PHARUS.
> *Ringing them Bells!*

> CHOIR.
> *I hear rocking in the land*
> *and ringing them bells.*

(Shift.)

THE QUAD

HEADMASTER. I want to speak to you.
PHARUS. Headmaster Marrow …
HEADMASTER. You throw Bobby out?
PHARUS. The Choir?
He just told you that?
That was months ago.
HEADMASTER. Why?
PHARUS. Now you know I'm not supposed to tattle on

A fellow student like that. But it was well within
My rights as lead of the Drew Prep Boys Choir.
If you would like sir I could go get the other members …
HEADMASTER. You think this is funny?
PHARUS. Like … Like Laugh out Loud?
HEADMASTER. You're smiling.
PHARUS. I am smiling but inside really I am hurt I …
I miss Bobby who else will interrupt me every
Time I give a correction to the choir.
HEADMASTER. I thought I asked you to tighten up.
No trouble!!!
PHARUS. What trouble, sir, every year a student either leaves or
Can't perform …
HEADMASTER. You are no longer lead of the choir.
PHARUS. Wh … what why?
HEADMASTER. You cannot lead. You can't get along with Choir
members then …
PHARUS. Oh sir … what am I gonna tell my mama?
HEADMASTER. Tell her …
PHARUS. That you took me off lead because your nephew
Called me a racial and a homophobic slur?
HEADMASTER. Excuse me?
PHARUS. I want an appeal.
HEADMASTER. What?
PHARUS. Is that the process?
HEADMASTER. Whose process?
PHARUS. I mean I don't know what the practice of the school
Is what the stance is for a student calling another student
A slur as it were but you know I just thought it un choir
Like, un cooperative. That's the only reason Bobby got
Kicked out.
HEADMASTER. When? I didn't … I will speak to Bobby.
PHARUS. But, sir, I'm still
Standing here being taken from one of the few, oh
So few, things that mean anything to me and I just …
Should I talk to the board of the school about it?
HEADMASTER. Pharus, are you threatening me?
PHARUS. I just want to lead the
Choir and I'm doing so well, why aren't you proud?
We sound great and all without

A sponsor. I did that Headmaster.
If I can do that without being called out my name …
HEADMASTER. Pharus, your wrist!
PHARUS. I'm sorry … Is my wrist the reason why I am being …
I mean it's a wrist a
Joint on my arm if the science teacher told me right
Can it really be doing … I mean is that why?
What!
HEADMASTER. Go … go to your room, Pharus
PHARUS. I won't be able to rest unless I know I can lead …
HEADMASTER. You … you are lead.
PHARUS. What say?
HEADMASTER. You are still lead, Pharus. *(Shift.)*

A HALL

MR. PENDLETON. No, no, David you can't … well you can but it's
Not very grounded. I understand what you were
Trying to do. Did you get some help from anyone
Like I said? I mean, listen, the topic is a hefty one,
The Rise of Capitalism and the Atlantic slave trade.
True the free market was hitting its stride on
The backs of chattel but you're not getting inside the
Process, you're not explaining the steps just horrifying
Us with numbers and it's true, terrifying, but you're taking it
Too personally.
DAVID. I'm Black.
MR. PENDLETON. Touché, young fella. Touché.
I … yes … um … "B" — ?
DAVID. Yeah, Thank you sir.
MR. PENDLETON. But listen try to take the other part of it
personally too,
Try to think larger. Not *just* the pain and suffering
But the pain the suffering *and* the calculating. That's the ugly
Part. People had to distance themselves, build a system that
Eliminated personhood in order to begin
Counting and thus writing people into jurisdiction as commodity.

As systems that supported the branding of
PHARUS. Four-fifths of a person.
MR. PENDLETON. Yes!
DAVID. But money was just the excuse.
PHARUS. How so?
DAVID. People been un-humanizing each other.
MR. PENDLETON. Dehumanizing.
DAVID. Dehumanizing each other in the name of land,
Customs and religion for centuries before. The rise
In personal wealth just made it more reachable.
MR. PENDLETON. Good ... very good. See That's better.
"A" minus,
You should have included that in the paper.
But I see once you get your discussion partner
Right *(Referring to Pharus.)* things just come out.
Very good. Good assist, Pharus.
Good, see this fellas, this is fun.
BOBBY. *Laissez les bon temps rouler!*
MR. PENDLETON. Let the good times roll!
Bobby you speak French?
BOBBY. I read it off a box.
MR. PENDLETON. Matches?
BOBBY. Condoms.
MR. PENDLETON. I ... uh ... AJ
You ready to come back to the Battle of Tours?
AJ. You like being in pain, Mr. P?
MR. PENDLETON. Pardon?
AJ. It hurt me to read it, I know it hurts you to hear it.
MR. PENDLETON. Come on fellas all I ask is that you keep engaging ...
PHARUS. Sir, I have a new topic.
BOBBY. Here he go.
PHARUS. "Spirituals: solely songs for the spirit."
I hope I don't upset anyone.
MR. PENDLETON. Now we're cooking: Let's hear it.
PHARUS. When I was little my grandmother would
Sing songs to me that she told me freed slaves. Not physically
But spiritually. She said "sangin'"
These songs deep in the night here
helped teach and coax other slaves, runaway and free

27

Into peace, serenity, let them know God was with them every
Where they went, gave them strength and spiritual nourishment.
Thus we call them Negro Spirituals.
She also would add, "they say these songs helped guide slaves
To freedom if they ran away … " Mapped out the geography and guided
Them through the night.
But with her shy self she would also say, "I don't know
About all that."
I always wondered about How she, "didn't know about
All that." Her admission of ignorance I later gathered was because
grandma wasn't There. She wasn't a slave and neither was her mother
and even
If she was, there was no way to pass down the direct understandin'
Of what a Negro spiritual like "Wade in the Water" meant to a slave
Who had just runaway. What she could verify by means of the right
Now was that these songs still gave her courage gave her strength
You could hear how "keep your hand on the plow"
Later became "keep your eyes on the prize"
And resulted in "yes we can … "
So rather than continuing to pass down these maybes to each other
Why do we never pass down what we know to be true? That
These songs forged in the shame and brutality of oppression are
Diamonds that glint and prove true that hope and love can live,
thrive, and even sing. There is no substantive proof that Spirituals
contain coded
Secret passageways to freedom. And I know some would condemn
Me for saying thus and breaking a long tradition of faith that we
Were creative enough, strong enough, to rebel even i' th' music that
Did oppress us. But the rhythm and the joy and the spiritual uplifting
That the music made, makes still, well; that is proof. That strength;
that is the rebellion.
For we left earthly things to the oppressors by way of this music
and we joined
The ranks of the heavenly host with its praise and love.
Thank you.
BOBBY. Just …
PHARUS. Thank you.
BOBBY. Like he just gave the state of the union address.
(Raises his hand.) I gotta question.

MR. PENDLETON. Bobby?

BOBBY. Who told you you could be the Negro Historian?

PHARUS. Oh …

BOBBY. I mean I am sure they got People smarter than you to look back on what
We've done and, and tell us what's
What.

PHARUS. All the proof is hearsay and guesstimations.

BOBBY. Guessta…?

AJ. Somebody thinks it's possible.

BOBBY. It's more than possible … Let me ask you something:
You stuck, somebody stole you away and got you
In chains you ain't gone try to get free?

PHARUS. I never said slaves didn't try and succeed in escaping.

DAVID. Even if it wasn't true …

BOBBY. It is true!

DAVID. I'm saying even if you can't prove it
Why would the theory exist this long?

BOBBY. Exactly!

DAVID. Must be some truth to it.

PHARUS. Think 'bout it David …
Black people were told in classrooms like this, but
Not, Mr. P would never, but we were
Taught our history, American or not, was shameful and
Ugly and anyone trying to rewrite themselves
Trying to come up from all that ugly would
File together, rub together any piece of anything
That might be true to make it over, to make
It better.

BOBBY. How you just gone say our ancestors made
Up stuff?

PHARUS. I'm not, you are. You're saying they intricately forged
Songs that had coded messages that told slaves how
To navigate the Mississippi, cross the Caribbean.

BOBBY. What you calling me a liar?

PHARUS. You know spirituals helped slaves to freedom?

BOBBY. Everybody know that, damn right

MR. PENDLETON. Bobby, I don't mind discussion: Language.

PHARUS. Tell me in "Swing Low, Sweet Chariot" where the message
Is. What does it mean exactly? Show me the proof?

29

BOBBY. It was to warn where the slave catchers were coming.
PHARUS. Well break it down for us? Or "Wade in the Water."
Why is the
Good God troubling the waters?
BOBBY. Meaning go in the waters 'cause the hounds can't pick up
your
Scent.
PHARUS. Oh so what song they used when there wasn't no hounds?

You don't know?
BOBBY. You don't know.
PHARUS. I never said I did. But when I don't know for sure
I don't make things up to fill it.
DAVID. Those songs were more than just …
PHARUS. See that's what I am talking about. Y'all keep saying
"More than just." What you mean? Without them being slave
Escape 007 plans they less than? Does anybody here
Love my Jesus?
Don't just diminish the song 'cause it might not be
A strategic map guiding slaves north. What they were and are is
Sweet honey in the rock that didn't just help the slaves
But Help us now, this day. I been in the church where
The girl with the sin on her heart or the man with the ailment
Found hope and a path 'cause of this music and it's
Those melodies the pitch harmonies and
Rhythms those are the maps and guides to the Promise
Land. Not on this earth but elsewhere in my
Father's house.
BOBBY. Huh.
MR. PENDLETON. Bobby where are you going? *(Bobby exits.)*
AJ. Let him go, sir.
DAVID. He just … He needs to cool off.
MR. PENDLETON. Alright. Alright. OK, who's next? *(Shift.)*

THE QUAD

BOBBY. Ain't you supposed to be in class?
JUNIOR. Aren't you?
BOBBY. Man, I had to get the hell out of there. *(Headmaster enters.)*
HEADMASTER. Junior, Bobby
BOBBY and JUNIOR. *(Sotto voce.)* Damn!
HEADMASTER. I've been looking for you.
BOBBY. I was just about to
Come to your office. You know this man letting …
HEADMASTER. Later. Hear me.
Tomorrow you are to report back to the choir room for rehearsal.
BOBBY. But …
HEADMASTER. Can you handle that?
BOBBY. Can I …
HEADMASTER. I'm not asking, I'm telling. Act up and see. This
is your cease and desist Order.
BOBBY. My…?
JUNIOR. Stop and don't do.
BOBBY. But Why?
HEADMASTER. What is with you students asking … You know in
My day that word wasn't even in your vocabulary
Unless you were in science class or reciting the alphabet?
Don't ask me Why! 'Cause I said so. Why, because
Unless you wanna Clean more quad I suggest you keep
Your mouth Shut until you sing at rehearsal tomorrow.
BOBBY. Huh.
HEADMASTER. What you say?
BOBBY. Nothing.

Nothing sir.
JUNIOR. Sir.
HEADMASTER. Get back to class. *(Headmaster exits.)*
BOBBY. Ain't this about a bi …
DAVID. You still at it out here?
JUNIOR. He stay mad don't he?
DAVID. Before I found the Lord I was the same way.

BOBBY. Huh, you still on that? This fool talking 'bout he
Gone be a pastor.
JUNIOR. That's cool.
BOBBY. How you gone be a pastor? You gotta graduate high school
Don't it?
DAVID. Wow, Bobby you on it hard today, man. You mad
At everybody 'cause you got bested boy?
BOBBY. Stch, that nigga ain't better than me!
DAVID. Huh, he better than me. This class kicking my ...
Taking my average down ...
BOBBY. Look how it's being run!
I heard Mr. P tell you, "Try Pharus he could show you
Interesting ways ... " You want Pharus to show you some things
David?
DAVID. Eh!
BOBBY. Oh so there you go that's what I'm talking about
You fired up too.
DAVID. Man, I ain't nothing.
BOBBY. You ought to be. You ought to be something you
Talking about you gone be a Pastor don't let
These sissies get you by association.
DAVID. What?
BOBBY. This Kat, he coming in here and talking about
Our music, our way and making it ... Making it
Extra! Everything just extra. This shit's pandemic.
DAVID. Endemic.
BOBBY. Him too. He changing shit and getting
Bold. I saw the way he draped 'cross you the other day.
DAVID. What?
BOBBY. "David hand me that book." Limp wrist.
Nasty nigga!
Calling our people liars. And they letting
Him. They allowing it. Ain't no way this near
Right.
I mean you supposed to be saved.
Called.
What's going on with
You!
DAVID. My man I'm trying to graduate. You know,
I got grades I need to keep. We ain't all paid for

Like you. Can't cuss the teacher out and leave class
Storm the halls and challenge everybody and expect
mama to still pay for ...
BOBBY. Eh!
Watch your mouth man, I know what you mean
We all got a game to play but watch yo mouth.
JUNIOR. Come on, fellas.
DAVID. I'm sorry man, I forgot she ... no disrespect.
BOBBY. I ain't asking you to get suspended man,
I'm just talking about association, careful who you walk
With.
DAVID. I walk with the Lord.
BOBBY. They say He didn't keep the best company either.
Look what they did to him. *(David is left alone. He begins to hum
and disrobe while ...)*

SOLUS

*The other Boys enter and prepare to Shower while listening at
some moments intensely and others not, to the Headmaster's
announcement.*

HEADMASTER. As the Good Book tells us, there is a season for
All things. We enter now into the middle ...
And in the middle season, Fall turning into harder
Winter, getting colder outside, I urge you all to find compassion
In your heart for each other. The tough of class, dropping
Low, now, weighing on some, the pressure of colleges to come,
Some of you are far from Home for the first time. And around now,
I know, I remember, it can get heavy. Look to your fellow Drew,
Older students, be a rock and remember who you are ...
We are Charles R. Drew Prep Proving Men for tomorrow. Showers;
Then quiet hour.

SHOWERS

DAVID.
Mmmm
Sometimes
I'm tossed and driven Lord
Sometimes I!
Don't know where to go.
My mother
My father
Won't own me. So I'll try to
To make heaven my home.

Sometimes I feel

Sometimes I feel like

BOYS.
Sometimes I feel like a
*   motherless child*

Sometimes I feel

Sometimes I feel like

Sometimes I feel like
*   a motherless child*

Sometimes I feel

Sometimes I feel like

Sometimes I feel like
*   a motherless child*

A long way from

BOBBY.
Sometimes ...

I feel

Like a motherless child

Sometimes ...

I feel

Like a motherless child

Sometimes ...

I feel

Like a motherless child

A long

34

A long way from

Long way from

From home

Sometimes I feel like I'm
a long way from home

Sometimes

I feel like

I feel

Sometimes I feel like

Like a motherless child.
JUNIOR.
I can hear my mother
calling me
She's calling me

I can hear her calling me

I can hear my mother's voice

I can hear her calling me

I can hear my mother's voice
And she's calling me, But I …

I can hear her call but I'm
a long way from home.
I can hear her calling me

I can hear my mother she's
calling me

I can hear her calling me

Oh, won't you come on home
child
Cross the waters

I can hear her call but I'm
a long way from Home

But I'm a long,
long way from home.
PHARUS.
Oh, True Believer!

True believer!

True believer!

True believer!

True believer!

True believer!

ALL.
Yes I'm a long way from home!

PHARUS.
True believer

BOYS.
True believer

True believer

True believer

True believer

True believer!

ALL.
True believer A long way
from home

(Singing ends abruptly. All exit save Pharus and AJ.)

AJ. Always got to be the best.

PHARUS. Was I singing too loud? I'm sorry you know
Sometimes I sing until the spirit moves in
My heart.

AJ. Yeah I heard.

You standing there or you taking a shower?

PHARUS. I'm trying to figure out how your penis is
That big.

AJ. Eh, Pharus!

PHARUS. I mean Lord you ain't but a lanky thang
How all that pressing like that?

AJ. You ... be quiet man.

PHARUS. Whoever you saving that for gone be sore.

AJ. Shoal will!

PHARUS. They better start doing stretches.

AJ. You getting bold boy, if somebody heard you talking like
That ...

PHARUS. What? I'm helping out science. I'ma get Mr. P to come
Over; this something out the prehistoric times. Need to
Be tagged and released back to the wild.

AJ. I know you complimenting me.

PHARUS. I just hope they ready for all that.

AJ. Why you always call it a pronoun?

PHARUS. Huh? You gots to use plain English I'm a man of
Music and numbers.

AJ. Every time you talk about who I might be with,

36

Who I might be interested in you call 'em "they"
You say, "them."
PHARUS. Do I do that?
AJ. You know what pronoun you should use, right?
You know who I'm saving or giving this and anything
Else to right ...
PHARUS. Huh.
AJ. She, a her.
PHARUS. I know.
AJ. Do you?
PHARUS. Yes. Why you being so serious?
AJ. Who you saving it for?
PHARUS. Oh me? Jesus.
AJ. I don't think Jesus interested.
PHARUS. Well I'm here for whatever he needs.
AJ. But what you need, Pharus? You need anything? *(David enters.)*
DAVID. Evening.
PHARUS. Oh Hey, David.
AJ. Sup David.
DAVID. I overheard y'all conversation Pharus
Sorry I just did but I'm sorry I just think
It's inappropriate, you know. Just for y'all
To be talking like that. In here I mean.
PHARUS. Oh I'm sorry David we thought ... I thought
Everyone was gone just teasing ... Anthony.
AJ. It's cool I'm done anyway.
PHARUS. Yeah I should shower.
Good night.
DAVID. God bless. *(Shift.)*

A HALL

HEADMASTER. Could you be the new faculty sponsor?
MR. PENDLETON. For the choir?
HEADMASTER. Yes.
MR. PENDLETON. But I'm ...
HEADMASTER. The right man for the job.

MR. PENDLETON. And can't sing.

HEADMASTER. Fine.

MR. PENDLETON. I'm ... me?

HEADMASTER. Yeah. He respects you.

MR. PENDLETON. Who?

HEADMASTER. Pharus. They all do.

MR. PENDLETON. He respects you too,
And I can't teach music, I'm just a ...

HEADMASTER. The choir isn't a class.

MR. PENDLETON. I know that but ...

HEADMASTER. Mr. Pendleton I just need you to be The peace maker can you do that?
You know the history of the choir, of the music?
It means so much to ... well everyone.
The choir has always had the more formal feeling but Pharus is breaking that
Somehow, it's ... an event to hear them. That's the choir we have been waiting
For. I mean they sound ... Did you hear them at Homecoming?

MR. PENDLETON. Fantastic!

HEADMASTER. Yes! Can you imagine that sound, from that few?
But they need adult supervision especially with Bobby
Rejoining the choir.

MR. PENDLETON. He left?

HEADMASTER. Pharus put him out, I put him back in.

MR. PENDLETON. I thought you said you wanted me to make peace?
They hate each other.

HEADMASTER. So I've seen. But it might look ... Bad
If I can ... A lot of people on the board, including my brother
Saw that my nephew was not in the choir at Homecoming.
And it might look badly if it appears I can't keep
Everyone including my own in line. It's my second year of tenure, sir,
And it's a financially
Risky year for the school. With the annual gala
We need everything, everyone
On board for the next 50 years to come. You know ...

MR. PENDLETON. I do.

HEADMASTER. Just ... Just watch them for me, please.

MR. PENDLETON. Alright.

HEADMASTER. Watch 'em. *(Shift.)*

A ROOM

AJ. Why are you being so mean?
PHARUS. All I ask Anthony is you leave your funky socks
On your side of the room. That's all I say, that's
It. I don't care if you leave papers and even your dusty
Draws on the floor but your socks smell like your shoes
Your shoes smell like your feet and yah feet smell
Like baby puke 'n' corn chips!
You laughing but then you got the nerve, My God,
To leave lil sticky packages when you think I ain't
Noticing, on these dangerously dirty socks, on my
Side of the room. I don't want your kith and kin cloth
On my things boy! I know you hear me.
AJ. Pharus Bwoi Calm down!
PHARUS. I AM! BEING! CALM!
AJ. What's wrong sweetheart?
PHARUS. Don't you call me …
AJ. You acting like my wife or something.
PHARUS. Uh, uh 'cause wives get some joy out of this lunacy.
I am just your roommate, barely your friend.
AJ. You my friend.
PHARUS. You wanna see a friendship end lil drummer boi?
Keep leaving these gifts 'round … in …
In fact you know what …
AJ. Pharus what you … don't … eh boi … you give me my sock.
PHARUS. Oh now you want your sock.
AJ. I'm not playing don't put my sock in that …
PHARUS. You bad, come get it.
AJ. Don't set my socks on … is you crazy boi!
PHARUS. Hah!
AJ. Oh, see now I'm gone fuck you up.
PHARUS. Now, Anthony, I just had to show you the consequence …
AJ. I got your consequence.
PHARUS. It was our rule.

AJ. Uh huh …
PHARUS. No stop now get offa me I can't stand
AJ. Yeah you don't like that.
PHARUS. Get offa me clown!
AJ. Yeah, now I'ma have to tickle!
PHARUS. No! No tickling! I can't! no … your thick club
man hands you are … *(Laughing.)* Stop! Anthony!
No horse play that's the rules …
You! *(Laughing.)* No ah ah ah ah! *(AJ wrestles Pharus down and tickles him more. AJ holds him between his legs pinning him and tickles and punches more. Pharus becomes aroused and screams.)*
ANTHONY!
AJ. Whoa what's wrong? What's wrong man, I hurt you?
PHARUS. Stay over there, AJ.
AJ. You don't never call me no AJ! What's wrong?
PHARUS. Just stay there please, don't come over
Here.
AJ. Tell me what happened, you want me to get
Somebody?
PHARUS. No!

No, I'm just … I'm …
AJ. Why you … Oh … Aw shit. I'm … I'm sorry man.
PHARUS. I … Oh my God …
AJ. Don't go man. It ain't … You can't help that, man.
I mean. Don't be doing that shit over me, but you …
I guess if a chick was … I mean you must be pent up
Or something, I ain't never caught you even …
PHARUS. Please! *(Beat.)*
Don't tell nobody.
AJ. I … c'mon, Pharus.

PHARUS. If you … If you want to leave …
I can say to people that …
AJ. What?
PHARUS. I know some juniors on your team said one day
I overheard them say,
They didn't know why you was in a room with a …
Someone like me … and that they wouldn't mind bunking
Their beds to make room … make room for you.

AJ. Roomie …
PHARUS. That wouldn't hurt my feelings, I understand.
Just don't tell …
AJ. You want me to go?
PHARUS. You wanna go?
AJ. I ain't say that. You kicking me out?
PHARUS. No. I …

Just … I need … Can you just give me a second, Anthony
I need to … I need to change my …
AJ. Yeah. *(About to leave. Then.)*
Pharus?
PHARUS. Hm.
AJ. When I came in second year … You were alone in here.
Who was your roommate? Who had moved out before? *(Shift.)*

A HALL

The boys and Mr. Pendleton enter the space. They all sit at the same time and stare for a long duration. Mr. Pendleton breaks the ice.

MR. PENDLETON. This is tense.
BOBBY. What?
PHARUS. Tense: another word for edginess, a stiff rigidity.
BOBBY. Must be something sensitive people feel.
PHARUS. Junior, spell sensitive?
BOBBY. Why you picking on him?
JUNIOR. Stch. I can spell …
PHARUS. Say if you wanna hurt a man hurt the thing
He loves.
JUNIOR. S-E-N — S … Sensa?
BOBBY. You coming out your mouth!
JUNIOR. … Damn
DAVID. Let's just rehearse.

41

AJ. Right, man, the Gala.

BOBBY. Huh, I'm not singing that new-age gospel sh …

MR. PENDLETON. The show is cancelled.

ALL THE BOYS. What?

MR. PENDLETON. As it stands, right now, you all can't act accordingly

Can't act like brothers, I mean … you know,

You know what I mean you can't act like a choir

Then you can't perform.

PHARUS. You can't …

AJ. Mr. P —

BOBBY. You can't cancel the Gala.

DAVID. School has to raise money.

PHARUS. Yeah.

MR. PENDLETON. Oh I know. But see I am sponsor of the choir now

And I'll just say they, meaning you, couldn't

Get it together. Therefore couldn't perform.

Which wouldn't be a lie. Would it? *(Junior moves to leave.)*

Sit down.

JUNIOR. Why do we have to stay if we aren't rehearsing?

MR. PENDLETON. We are. We are. Um … for the next week

Or so I would like you have to as … as punishment

For your behavior you all have to bring in a song

From your childhood … No from your parents' childhood

That you heard or know or … or … Learn it! This is

A school, let's try that. Get i-mail or g-tunes and download

A song from your parents' repertoire no spiritual

Or gospel. It can be a slow jam or something from

The quiet storm, you know from the grown and sexy

AJ. Alright, Mr. P!

PHARUS. Talking about grown and sexy!

MR. PENDLETON. Alright, alright you know what I mean. Bring it …

Bring it in and sing it … for each other.

DAVID. Perform it?

MR. PENDLETON. That's right.

As best you can. Okay?

And then we'll rehearse for the Gala, which is back on if you

Get this assignment done agreed?
Get out. *(All exit. Pharus trails.)*
PHARUS. Nice one.
MR. PENDLETON. Oh thanks.
PHARUS. Yeah.
Next time put a lil bass in your voice
You know, just show 'em you mean it.
MR. PENDLETON. Alright. *(Lowers voice.)* Alright. *(Shift.)*

CALL HOME

Junior hums.

PHARUS. I know, I know Mama … I'm not going to embarrass
anybody.
It will be good. Maybe … I don't know if I am going to
Be singing this year.
I just called to say, "hey," really. I mean it's getting close
I didn't even really believe it would happen
I mean I did, I know you would have killed me but …
Mama that's not Christian. Or ladylike. I'm sorry
I'm not trying to tell you how to be a woman. What?
I … right … right. He's good. He asked about you the other
Day. No that's, that's, David he's the one going to be
A minister. Anthony is my roommate. On the … right
On the baseball team. Mama please don't let nobody catch
You saying that Anthony is a phyne ass lil boy. They will!
They will put you in jail. No … I don't know what they doing for
Graduation prolly just walking like I is … I am.
You … you coming, right? I know you got a lot but I
Just asked. Right you don't have to be here to
Know I graduated. Hope you proud. You will be …
You will be.

A HALL

*Bobby and Junior sing a secular song from the eighties, like by an artist such as New Edition.**

MR. PENDLETON. That was lovely!
What's that song called,
Fellas?
PHARUS. *[Title of the song.]*
MR. PENDLETON. Very good Junior and Bobby see this is fun!
AJ. Fun.
MR. PENDLETON. Alright, who's next?
PHARUS. I mean just have a question.
BOBBY. Lord …
MR. PENDLETON. Oh, Go ahead.
PHARUS. How old IS your mama Bobby?
BOBBY. What?
AJ. Pharus!
PHARUS. What?
I mean that song came out in what '88 or something
I mean if your mama was listening
To this song in her child hood she musta' had you when
She was what 16, 17. Ooh she was a ol' fast one.
BOBBY. Nigga …
MR. PENDLETON. Hey!
BOBBY. Say something else 'bout my mama …
JUNIOR. Pharus don't …
AJ. Just stand down
PHARUS. I'm just saying Bobby calm down all our mamas had
To drop it low and pick it up slow for us to get here.
BOBBY. *(In his face.)* She dead you punk-ass nigga!
MR. PENDLETON. Eh, I don't care I don't care how mad.
Do NOT use that word here!
PHARUS. I'm sorry, I'm so sorry …
DAVID. Pharus stop talking.

* See Special Note on Songs and Recordings on copyright page.

PHARUS. No I'm just apologizing I didn't know Bobby sincerely
How old was she when she passed?
BOBBY. That's…!
AJ. Hold up.
BOBBY. You leave my mama out your mouth, you faggot ass
Nigga!
MR. PENDLETON. *(Jacks Bobby up.)* Damnit! Hey! You listen,
you listen!
I told … I told you not to say that word again. I mean it.
I mean it, damnit, It is ugly don't say it! Stop saying it!
AJ. Whoa.
PHARUS. Mr. P calm down.
MR. PENDLETON. I will not be calm. You're in this too. You
can't be civil
And then you calling each other words you don't know
Anything about.
BOBBY. What you know 'bout it?
MR. PENDLETON. I know I've lost enough friends behind that
word.
Rehearsal is over.
Get the hell out of here. *(Shift.)*

SHOWER

Junior comes forward to sing.

JUNIOR.
  There is a fountain filled with Blood
  Drawn from Emmanuel's veins;
  And sinners plunged beneath that flood
  Lose all their guilty stains.
  Lose all their guilty stains;
  Lose all their guilty …

  The dying thief rejoiced to see
  That fountain in his day

And there may I, though vile as he,
Wash all my sins away!
Wash all my sins away!

Oooooh
Oooooh
Oooooh

(Enter Pharus in a towel. He walks towards a shower. Water is running.
Who he is speaking to is unseen by us.)
PHARUS. I just wanted to say sorry about earlier.
It was never meant to upset the whole rehearsal like
That. I am sure words got spoken wasn't meant
To come out the way they do. Maybe I talk too much
I'm just ... I don't really. Just been
Thinking about it all day, and that
Look on your face. You must think I'm some
Kind of ... I ... I went too far. And
I'm sorry to you,
I ... don't ...
Know what I'm saying. I'm more so just standing here
Like I do, sometimes.
Like we do.
I don't think anyone else
Is near, or can ... but all day I just been hoping to stand
Here.
Is that alright?
You know I like standing
By you. And sometimes you like it too. Can I ...
Should I stand a lil closer ...
Huh?
You tell me ...
You tell me when. *(Pharus walks until he is unseen by us. Sound of a*
door opening, Junior enters the space. Sound of a punch hitting a face.
Pharus falls onto the stage holding his face. Shift.)

THE QUAD

DAVID. Mr P.
MR. PENDLETON. David.
DAVID. Hey I wanted to …
MR. PENDLETON. I don't really feel like talking to you fellas.
DAVID. I know sir, and I'm sorry about … I really
I wanted to turn in my assignment.
MR. PENDLETON. Leave it until Monday. You won't be
marked down.
DAVID. No, not the class, the song … the song for Choir.
MR. PENDLETON. David … what … out here?
DAVID. Yes sir.
MR. PENDLETON. You're wet.
DAVID. Yes sir.
… I would like to sing the
Song that I would have sung, Mr. P, had Bobby
And Pharus not … Not got into an argument. I wondered if that
Would be alright with you? Please.
MR. PENDLETON. David why are you … are you alright?
DAVID. No sir, *(David sings a song such as "Love Ballad" by
L.T.D.* Shift.)*

AN OFFICE

HEADMASTER. What happened?
Son?
I know you might be ashamed.
I know that. None
Of the boys … no boy on this campus has
A nick on 'em. 'Cept you, son. Tell me about
The fight.
PHARUS. Wan't a fight.

---
* See Special Note on Songs and Recordings on copyright page.

HEADMASTER. So, what, you fell?

PHARUS. Fight mean you put hands up and fight
Back. I just … just took it.

HEADMASTER. Why … why would you do that?

PHARUS. What you fight for, sir? What you fight
For? You fight when you believe what
You doing, what you are, is right. Huh.
Everybody 'round you always telling you, showing
You that you ain't nothing, that they don't
Want you to be nothing, what you fight
For then? What you defending?
You believe like, like they believe so
Who you fighting for?

HEADMASTER. Don't … don't cry, Pharus.

PHARUS. I fell. I fell in the showers.

HEADMASTER. Don't lie …

PHARUS. I did!

HEADMASTER. The custodian found you laying on that side.
The bruise on your eye and lip on this side
Pharus just say who …

PHARUS. No! No.
Ain't nobody done nothing.

HEADMASTER. Stop lying.

PHARUS. You stop calling me a liar and I will
Stop being one.
I'm a Drew man. You wanna holla out something
'Bout me, can't you say that, Headmaster?
You see I'm low need something to lift
My head into, try that. Pharus is a Drew man …

HEADMASTER. Son.

PHARUS. He lives the Drew way.

HEADMASTER. Stop.

PHARUS. He follows the Drew rules.

HEADMASTER. That rule was made up amongst students
This, this is a real matter.

PHARUS. Would you rather be feared or respected Headmaster
Marrow?

HEADMASTER. Pharus …

PHARUS. Which!

HEADMASTER. I … I … respected.

PHARUS. I can't ever make them fear me. *(Shift.)*

AN OFFICE

AJ sits.

HEADMASTER. Anthony …
AJ. My first year was your first year Headmaster,
Remember?
HEADMASTER. I remember.
AJ. I came in a sophomore,
My family came up that open house, they came up to see
The school and classes and my room. They came in and
Shook hands with Pharus. My brother, my older brother,
Waited 'til Pharus was gone and turned t' my mama and say
"Why you letting AJ room with a faggot." Talking 'bout Pharus,
"He don't need to room with no chump. You better check who
Anthony is staying up here with. You better check what's going
On." Talkin' 'bout this silly, nice kid … who had been loaning me
Supplies since start 'cause we couldn't afford 'em.
And he ask me every day, every day since "If I needed help with
anything … "
and here go my brother.
My only Brother.
"Better check who Anthony is staying with."
Pharus came in and said goodbye to my mother. He made
Her laugh at something, and they left.
He heard what my brother said about him though.
He kept talking to me but looking away
Like he was apologizing for something.
I wanted to tell him, "Pharus
Don't you … don't you look down.
You been nicer to me than my
Blood ever, boy, don't you look down.
Pick your head up boy. Up."
But I ain't say anything.

49

I just let him look.
Ain't seen that face on him in long time, ain't seen it until now,
Headmaster. 'Til he come in with that black and purple all over his
face. And looking down. Like he saying … sorry. Sorry for what?
Nah I ain't hit him sir,
Only way I Hit him if I could knock that sorry off his face. *(Shift.)*

AN OFFICE

Bobby sits.

BOBBY. No … No … See I knew … No.
HEADMASTER. Bobby …
BOBBY. Sir.
HEADMASTER. Shut up. Sit down.
BOBBY. I'm saying Un … Headmaster Marrow I ain't
I didn't do anything.
HEADMASTER. So why are you squirming your face up so?
BOBBY. 'Cause I knew you would drag me in here …
HEADMASTER. You speak too much son, you need to
Know when to be quiet.
JUNIOR. I tell him that all the time.
HEADMASTER. Why are you here Junior?
JUNIOR. I'm his witness.
HEADMASTER. To?
BOBBY. Me not punching the shit outta Pharus.
HEADMASTER. I don't care what he's here to do I know
You are not gone talk like that, not here.
I've
Heard …
About what you said …
What you said in front of Mr. Pendleton!
BOBBY. He told you how he jacked me up?
HEADMASTER. I oughta jack you up! Boy! Do you know that
Man marched with Dr. King and sat in more
Sit ins than you have years of life and you sitting

50

Your silly ass in front of him spouting off
Like Kanye at a press conference! Man came
In talking 'bout he wanted to retire again. Talking
'Bout he don't know what the youth are coming
To, doesn't know if he is helping us impact our
People. This man sitting in my office talking to
Me about this and my nephew, my blood and ...
BOBBY. It wasn't me. Right Junior, tell him.
JUNIOR. Huh?
BOBBY. Tell him.
JUNIOR. He went over to the Public school band practice.
HEADMASTER. You were off campus when Pharus got hit?
BOBBY. Yes.
HEADMASTER. You were supposed to be showering and lights out.
JUNIOR. Right, but he wasn't. He left the showers and went there ...
HEADMASTER. To do what?
JUNIOR. Be with his girl.
BOBBY. You ain't have to say all that.
JUNIOR. You wanted me to say it, I'ma say it all.
I usually look out to make sure nobody caught 'em.
I've been look out every time he's gone. He want me
To go this time. I stayed. I ... They
Use condoms and she says she's on the pill.
HEADMASTER. I ... I ...
JUNIOR. She moans a lot and winks at me. He goes quick
And breathes hard.
HEADMASTER. Stop please.
This is ... what is wrong with you all? *(Shift.)*

AN OFFICE

David sits.

DAVID. We are fearfully and marvelously made, sir.
HEADMASTER. I don't ...

DAVID. Psalms 139. Say it was written by King
David, say he was down, had turned from the Lord
And he wrote it crying out for forgiveness. I ...
Just found it,
"Fearfully and marvelously are we made."
HEADMASTER. David.
DAVID. Say he had just fought a fight he shouldn't have,
Shed some blood he wasn't supposed to and wrote
These words that's what they say in the you know the
Scholarly accounts or ...
I don't believe it, sir.
I don't believe this is a prayer for ... regret or remorse
Or whatever. I think he's ... I think he's surprised at who
He is ... who he really is.
I think he's looking down blood on his fingers and he saying,
"What am I Lord?"
What a marvelous and fearful thing am I?
Are all of us, sir.
HEADMASTER. David did you hit Pharus Young?
DAVID. I had prayed over it. So many times, just kept praying
On it. Every time it would happen.
HEADMASTER. Every time?
DAVID. And the Lord was silent. I mean when I got called
To be a minister I could feel the Spirit but when I was
Asking him to make this ... make it ... go away ...
He fell so quiet
And I ain't have nobody but Pharus. You understand, sir?
It was us alone in it sir until I thought I heard somebody come
In and ...
HEADMASTER. What are you saying son?
DAVID. I should have waited on the Lord.
I didn't look to see where it was leading until it was too late ...
HEADMASTER. You ...
DAVID. 'Til I looked at my hands and some of the blood spilling
was my own. *(Shift.)*

AN OFFICE

Mr. Pendleton and Headmaster Marrow are in the office.
Pharus is sitting outside with his head in his lap.

HEADMASTER. Was it this hard in your day?
MR. PENDLETON. Well ...
HEADMASTER. You can tell me. When the dust settled ...
MR. PENDLETON. I'm ...
HEADMASTER. When you didn't have to fight the Klan off the
campus.
MR. PENDLETON. What?
HEADMASTER. My Brothers used to tell me ... I think they
were trying to scare
Me before I came here. They used to say that the Headmaster
Had to stand in the threshold of the old building with a shotgun
'Cause the Klan was always threatening and burning ...
MR. PENDLETON. There was no Klan in this part of the ...
HEADMASTER. I knew they were lying.
MR. PENDLETON. But
You got your occasional friendly farmer though
Down the road who would post signs saying
All kinds of things. Some boys would stray
Off campus and come back a little roughed up
Sometimes shaken pretty badly.
HEADMASTER. Huh. That's not in the annals.
MR. PENDLETON. Do they ever read right? Is there anything in
there that really ...
Stephen?
HEADMASTER. Sir?
MR. PENDLETON. Are you really surprised?
HEADMASTER. I am ... Shocked.
MR. PENDLETON. This has been an all-male school for 49 ...
HEADMASTER. 50 years, sir.
MR. PENDLETON. And you never thought once ... once that
there could be ...

HEADMASTER. No, well I was prepared for … I mean …
If he had come in here …
MR. PENDLETON. Who, who he?
HEADMASTER. David.
MR. PENDLETON. Where is he?
HEADMASTER. Gone. Packed. Gone. Rule for fighting is suspension
Suspension means no scholarship. I told him Go
Home we can find a way to make up the money for
The last few weeks. But when his father found out …
MR. PENDLETON. You spoke to his father?
HEADMASTER. He did. He
Told him … I said … He could have said … huh.
Mr. Pendleton if that boy had said to me that he acted in self-defense …
MR. PENDLETON. What would you have done?
HEADMASTER. I would be fair. I would suspend them both and make sure
That we nipped that kind of behavior in the bud.
But I couldn't because my student came in here … Huh …
And told me he thought he was in …
What jurisdiction do I put on that?
MR. PENDLETON. I see, I see, you were preparing for someone to
Hurt Pharus?
HEADMASTER. Yes, no, well yes but no …
MR. PENDLETON. … Never thought someone could love him.

I don't have any advice for you, Stephen, I really don't but I will
Say this, in 49 … 50 … 50 years of this school, in the records or not,
This is not the First time "love" found this form.
Won't be the last.
You plan on staying Headmaster, well, I'd prepare for that.
HEADMASTER. Pharus has been outside my office all day.
MR. PENDLETON. I saw.
HEADMASTER. He keeps swearing that he won't tell if I just let
David stay. After all that he's still looking out for his fellow Drew.
MR. PENDLETON. Are you going to tell him … about the choir,
I mean.
That he can't perform?
HEADMASTER. How do I …
MR. PENDLETON. Not much has changed. Boys with black
eyes weren't allowed to lead choir back then either. *(Shift.)*

CALL HOME

HEADMASTER.
I been in the storm so long!
I been in the storm so long
  children
Been in the storm so long.
Give me lil time to pray.

I been	BOYS.
in the storm so Long	*Ooooh*
I been in the storm so long	*Ooooh*
Children	*Ooooh*
Been in the storm so long	*Ooooh*
Give me lil time to pray.	*Ooooh*
Lord	*Ooooh*
Give me a lil time to pray.	*Ooooh Ooooh Ooooh*
Ooooh Ooooh Ooooh Ooooh	
Give me a lil time to pray.	

A ROOM

PHARUS. *(Starting to sing.)*
  When we walk …
AJ. Pharus?
PHARUS. Were you sleep?
AJ. What are you doing?
PHARUS. I'm …
AJ. I mean I *was* sleep.
PHARUS. I haven't practiced in so long, the Headmaster tomorrow, might change his mind. He might …
AJ. Pharus …
PHARUS. I mean it's a chance, right?
AJ. You need some sleep

PHARUS. I can't.

AJ. You ain't slept or said much o' nothing since …

PHARUS. It was hard to, jaw was all jacked up …

AJ. That's not funny.

PHARUS. It ain't cute either but I can still sound good.

AJ. Pharus graduation's tomorrow ain't that enough?

PHARUS. Ask my mama.

AJ. She here?

PHARUS. Yeah.

AJ. She came.

PHARUS. Couldn't even look at me. Didn't say nothing
'Bout my … face. Just said, "You need a haircut.
Ain't no barbers round here?" She know I don't
Set foot in nobody's Barber shop.

AJ. Let me hook you up.

PHARUS. You got your clippers?

AJ. I'm from Willacoochie, GA you know I stay with a set of Andis
on me.

PHARUS. Just so country.

AJ. C'mon hold this sheet round. I'll line you up.
How come you don't let the barber cut it?

PHARUS. Huh. My friend Kevin used to go with me all the time.
When I was little.
My mama would tell me to get my hair cut 'cause,
"You looking too pretty."
Me and Kevin would walk to the corner shop and …
All these grown men would sit there
talking about, some of the, to this day, stupidest
Shit.

AJ. Pharus! *(Laughing.)* Hold still.

PHARUS. I'm sorry …

AJ. I'm proud of you. I ain't never heard you cuss.

PHARUS. People acting like Barbershops this vessel of great
conversation and debate for
Black people and here these bastards talking 'bout PlayStation 8 and
Crash Death Auto and watching the worst movies … bought from
some man who come 'round with a book a DVDs. And then
complaining that the movie's bad quality. Talking 'bout, "*The
MAN keeping us down*"
Meanwhile they watching *Baby Daddy's Little Girl 3* on the bootleg

My God! — Ooh see, look at the devil in my shando. Praise Break.
(AJ laughs.)
I never felt right there. Never.
Always felt like the last place
I should be, and they made sure I knew it.
They loved Kevin, though. He was gone be something.
A ball player or something. One time I told
Kevin, reminded him, in my way, Kevin your
Mama said you suppose to get a crovonics.
AJ. The fuck is that?
PHARUS. Lady meant a "*quo vadis*," *he* knew it meant
"Short and simple" and he up there telling the
Barber he wanna fade with a clean taper and
A "K" on the side. I say, "Kevin that ain't what your
Mama say." Kevin looked at me like spit would've been too kind,
Like hell was a place. He walked up on me say,
"Don't tell me nothing you faggot. Don't you
Say nothing to me."
Messed up, though. Made the mistake of looking up after he said that,
Looked 'round for a place to run and all these men, the barber too
All of them, grown, looking at me, what was
I 8 or 9? Looking at me like, "That's right,"
Like,
"That's what you get."
Like they were all with him and not no one …
Couldn't even walk in that barbershop
Told my Mama I was cutting my own hair to help her save money.
Every place I went felt the same. 'Cept …
Until I got to Drew. Everybody didn't like me but
I had … I had space to let me be. That was what was
Good about being here.
Now everywhere everybody looking like, "That's what you get."
AJ. You cool?
PHARUS. It does look a little better Anthony, thank you.
AJ. Think we should get to sleep.
PHARUS. Yeah.
AJ. You should sleep.
PHARUS. Okay, I'ma try.

AJ. Here.

Sleep here.
PHARUS. Thank you.
AJ. That's what you get. *(Shift.)*

BOBBY and JUNIOR.
> *I got a rainbow*
> *Tied all 'round my shoulder, huh*

ALL BOYS.
> *I got a rainbow*
> *Tied all 'round my shoulder, huh*
> *I'm goin' home,*
> *My Lord, I'm goin' home,*
> *Ev'rywhere I, huh, sss*
> *Where I look this morning,*
> *Ev'rywhere I, huh, sss*
> *Where I look this morning,*
> *Look like rain, Lord*

BOBBY and PHARUS.
> *My Lord,*

AJ and JUNIOR.
> *My Lord look like rain,*

BOBBY and PHARUS.
> *My Lord look like rain*

AJ and JUNIOR.
> *Mama say come home*

BOBBY and PHARUS.
> *Mama say come home*
> *Come home*

AJ and JUNIOR.
> *My Lord son, come home*

ALL BOYS.
> *Mama say come home*

BOBBY and PHARUS.
> *My Lord*

AJ and JUNIOR.
> *My Lord*

ALL BOYS.
> *Son come home*

AJ.
I got a rainbow
JUNIOR.
I got a rainbow
BOBBY.
I got a rainbow
PHARUS.
I got a rainbow
ALL BOYS.
Tied all 'round my shoulder,
Mama say come home,
My Lord son, come home
(Shift.)

COMMENCEMENT/EPILOGUE

HEADMASTER. Ladies and Gentlemen, family and friends, Welcome to the 50th anniversary Commencement for the Charles R. Drew Prep School for Boys. And now to present the school song next year's
Choir Lead. Mr. Bobby Marrow.
(Lights up on Bobby. He steps forward and sings, "Trust and Obey," the school's Song.)
BOBBY.
When we walk with the Lord
in the light of His Word,
what a glory He sheds on our way!
While we do His good will,
He abides with us still,
and with all who will trust and obey.
Trust and obey, for there's no other way
to be happy in Jesus,
(At this moment Bobby stops singing the school song and looks behind as Pharus did a year ago. He turns and continues.)
But to trust and obey.
(Lights.)

End of Play

PROPERTY LIST

Pitch pipe
Socks
Hair clippers

NEW PLAYS

★ MOTHERHOOD OUT LOUD by Leslie Ayvazian, Brooke Berman, David Cale, Jessica Goldberg, Beth Henley, Lameece Issaq, Claire LaZebnik, Lisa Loomer, Michele Lowe, Marco Pennette, Theresa Rebeck, Luanne Rice, Annie Weisman and Cheryl L. West, conceived by Susan R. Rose and Joan Stein. When entrusting the subject of motherhood to such a dazzling collection of celebrated American writers, what results is a joyous, moving, hilarious, and altogether thrilling theatrical event. "Never fails to strike both the funny bone and the heart." –*BackStage*. "Packed with wisdom, laughter, and plenty of wry surprises." –*TheaterMania*. [1M, 3W] ISBN: 978-0-8222-2589-8

★ COCK by Mike Bartlett. When John takes a break from his boyfriend, he accidentally meets the girl of his dreams. Filled with guilt and indecision, he decides there is only one way to straighten this out. "[A] brilliant and blackly hilarious feat of provocation." –*Independent*. "A smart, prickly and rewarding view of sexual and emotional confusion." –*Evening Standard*. [3M, 1W] ISBN: 978-0-8222-2766-3

★ F. Scott Fitzgerald's THE GREAT GATSBY adapted for the stage by Simon Levy. Jay Gatsby, a self-made millionaire, passionately pursues the elusive Daisy Buchanan. Nick Carraway, a young newcomer to Long Island, is drawn into their world of obsession, greed and danger. "Levy's combination of narration, dialogue and action delivers most of what is best in the novel." –*Seattle Post-Intelligencer*. "A beautifully crafted interpretation of the 1925 novel which defined the Jazz Age." –*London Free Press*. [5M, 4W] ISBN: 978-0-8222-2727-4

★ LONELY, I'M NOT by Paul Weitz. At an age when most people are discovering what they want to do with their lives, Porter has been married and divorced, earned seven figures as a corporate "ninja," and had a nervous breakdown. It's been four years since he's had a job or a date, and he's decided to give life another shot. "Critic's pick!" –*NY Times*. "An enjoyable ride." –*NY Daily News*. [3M, 3W] ISBN: 978-0-8222-2734-2

★ ASUNCION by Jesse Eisenberg. Edgar and Vinny are not racist. In fact, Edgar maintains a blog condemning American imperialism, and Vinny is three-quarters into a Ph.D. in Black Studies. When Asuncion becomes their new roommate, the boys have a perfect opportunity to demonstrate how open-minded they truly are. "Mr. Eisenberg writes lively dialogue that strikes plenty of comic sparks." –*NY Times*. "An almost ridiculously enjoyable portrait of slacker trauma among would-be intellectuals." –*Newsday*. [2M, 2W] ISBN: 978-0-8222-2630-7

DRAMATISTS PLAY SERVICE, INC.
440 Park Avenue South, New York, NY 10016 212-683-8960 Fax 212-213-1539
postmaster@dramatists.com   www.dramatists.com

NEW PLAYS

★ **THE PICTURE OF DORIAN GRAY by Roberto Aguirre-Sacasa, based on the novel by Oscar Wilde.** Preternaturally handsome Dorian Gray has his portrait painted by his college classmate Basil Hallwood. When their mutual friend Henry Wotton offers to include it in a show, Dorian makes a fateful wish—that his portrait should grow old instead of him—and strikes an unspeakable bargain with the devil. [5M, 2W] ISBN: 978-0-8222-2590-4

★ **THE LYONS by Nicky Silver.** As Ben Lyons lies dying, it becomes clear that he and his wife have been at war for many years, and his impending demise has brought no relief. When they're joined by their children all efforts at a sentimental goodbye to the dying patriarch are soon abandoned. "Hilariously frank, clear-sighted, compassionate and forgiving." –*NY Times.* "Mordant, dark and rich." –*Associated Press.* [3M, 3W] ISBN: 978-0-8222-2659-8

★ **STANDING ON CEREMONY by Mo Gaffney, Jordan Harrison, Moisés Kaufman, Neil LaBute, Wendy MacLeod, José Rivera, Paul Rudnick, and Doug Wright, conceived by Brian Shnipper.** Witty, warm and occasionally wacky, these plays are vows to the blessings of equality, the universal challenges of relationships and the often hilarious power of love. "CEREMONY puts a human face on a hot-button issue and delivers laughter and tears rather than propaganda." –*BackStage.* [3M, 3W] ISBN: 978-0-8222-2654-3

★ **ONE ARM by Moisés Kaufman, based on the short story and screenplay by Tennessee Williams.** Ollie joins the Navy and becomes the lightweight boxing champion of the Pacific Fleet. Soon after, he loses his arm in a car accident, and he turns to hustling to survive. "[A] fast, fierce, brutally beautiful stage adaptation." –*NY Magazine.* "A fascinatingly lurid, provocative and fatalistic piece of theater." –*Variety.* [7M, 1W] ISBN: 978-0-8222-2564-5

★ **AN ILIAD by Lisa Peterson and Denis O'Hare.** A modern-day retelling of Homer's classic. Poetry and humor, the ancient tale of the Trojan War and the modern world collide in this captivating theatrical experience. "Shocking, glorious, primal and deeply satisfying." –*Time Out NY.* "Explosive, altogether breathtaking." –*Chicago Sun-Times.* [1M] ISBN: 978-0-8222-2687-1

★ **THE COLUMNIST by David Auburn.** At the height of the Cold War, Joe Alsop is the nation's most influential journalist, beloved, feared and courted by the Washington world. But as the '60s dawn and America undergoes dizzying change, the intense political dramas Joe is embroiled in become deeply personal as well. "Intensely satisfying." –*Bloomberg News.* [5M, 2W] ISBN: 978-0-8222-2699-4

DRAMATISTS PLAY SERVICE, INC.
440 Park Avenue South, New York, NY 10016 212-683-8960 Fax 212-213-1539
postmaster@dramatists.com www.dramatists.com

NEW PLAYS

★ **BENGAL TIGER AT THE BAGHDAD ZOO by Rajiv Joseph.** The lives of two American Marines and an Iraqi translator are forever changed by an encounter with a quick-witted tiger who haunts the streets of war-torn Baghdad. "[A] boldly imagined, harrowing and surprisingly funny drama." –*NY Times.* "Tragic yet darkly comic and highly imaginative." –*CurtainUp.* [5M, 2W] ISBN: 978-0-8222-2565-2

★ **THE PITMEN PAINTERS by Lee Hall, inspired by a book by William Feaver.** Based on the triumphant true story, a group of British miners discover a new way to express themselves and unexpectedly become art-world sensations. "Excitingly ambiguous, in-the-moment theater." –*NY Times.* "Heartfelt, moving and deeply politicized." –*Chicago Tribune.* [5M, 2W] ISBN: 978-0-8222-2507-2

★ **RELATIVELY SPEAKING by Ethan Coen, Elaine May and Woody Allen.** In TALKING CURE, Ethan Coen uncovers the sort of insanity that can only come from family. Elaine May explores the hilarity of passing in GEORGE IS DEAD. In HONEYMOON MOTEL, Woody Allen invites you to the sort of wedding day you won't forget. "Firecracker funny." –*NY Times.* "A rollicking good time." –*New Yorker.* [8M, 7W] ISBN: 978-0-8222-2394-8

★ **SONS OF THE PROPHET by Stephen Karam.** If to live is to suffer, then Joseph Douaihy is more alive than most. With unexplained chronic pain and the fate of his reeling family on his shoulders, Joseph's health, sanity, and insurance premium are on the line. "Explosively funny." –*NY Times.* "At once deep, deft and beautifully made." –*New Yorker.* [5M, 3W] ISBN: 978-0-8222-2597-3

★ **THE MOUNTAINTOP by Katori Hall.** A gripping reimagination of events the night before the assassination of the civil rights leader Dr. Martin Luther King, Jr. "An ominous electricity crackles through the opening moments." –*NY Times.* "[A] thrilling, wild, provocative flight of magical realism." –*Associated Press.* "Crackles with theatricality and a humanity more moving than sainthood." –*NY Newsday.* [1M, 1W] ISBN: 978-0-8222-2603-1

★ **ALL NEW PEOPLE by Zach Braff.** Charlie is 35, heartbroken, and just wants some time away from the rest of the world. Long Beach Island seems to be the perfect escape until his solitude is interrupted by a motley parade of misfits who show up and change his plans. "Consistently and sometimes sensationally funny." –*NY Times.* "A morbidly funny play about the trendy new existential condition of being young, adorable, and miserable." –*Variety.* [2M, 2W] ISBN: 978-0-8222-2562-1

DRAMATISTS PLAY SERVICE, INC.
440 Park Avenue South, New York, NY 10016 212-683-8960 Fax 212-213-1539
postmaster@dramatists.com www.dramatists.com

NEW PLAYS

★ **CLYBOURNE PARK by Bruce Norris.** WINNER OF THE 2011 PULITZER PRIZE AND 2012 TONY AWARD. Act One takes place in 1959 as community leaders try to stop the sale of a home to a black family. Act Two is set in the same house in the present day as the now predominantly African-American neighborhood battles to hold its ground. "Vital, sharp-witted and ferociously smart." –*NY Times.* "A theatrical treasure…Indisputably, uproariously funny." –*Entertainment Weekly.* [4M, 3W] ISBN: 978-0-8222-2697-0

★ **WATER BY THE SPOONFUL by Quiara Alegría Hudes.** WINNER OF THE 2012 PULITZER PRIZE. A Puerto Rican veteran is surrounded by the North Philadelphia demons he tried to escape in the service. "This is a very funny, warm, and yes uplifting play." –*Hartford Courant.* "The play is a combination poem, prayer and app on how to cope in an age of uncertainty, speed and chaos." –*Variety.* [4M, 3W] ISBN: 978-0-8222-2716-8

★ **RED by John Logan.** WINNER OF THE 2010 TONY AWARD. Mark Rothko has just landed the biggest commission in the history of modern art. But when his young assistant, Ken, gains the confidence to challenge him, Rothko faces the agonizing possibility that his crowning achievement could also become his undoing. "Intense and exciting." –*NY Times.* "Smart, eloquent entertainment." –*New Yorker.* [2M] ISBN: 978-0-8222-2483-9

★ **VENUS IN FUR by David Ives.** Thomas, a beleaguered playwright/director, is desperate to find an actress to play Vanda, the female lead in his adaptation of the classic sadomasochistic tale *Venus in Fur.* "Ninety minutes of good, kinky fun." –*NY Times.* "A fast-paced journey into one man's entrapment by a clever, vengeful female." –*Associated Press.* [1M, 1W] ISBN: 978-0-8222-2603-1

★ **OTHER DESERT CITIES by Jon Robin Baitz.** Brooke returns home to Palm Springs after a six-year absence and announces that she is about to publish a memoir dredging up a pivotal and tragic event in the family's history—a wound they don't want reopened. "Leaves you feeling both moved and gratifyingly sated." –*NY Times.* "A genuine pleasure." –*NY Post.* [2M, 3W] ISBN: 978-0-8222-2605-5

★ **TRIBES by Nina Raine.** Billy was born deaf into a hearing family and adapts brilliantly to his family's unconventional ways, but it's not until he meets Sylvia, a young woman on the brink of deafness, that he finally understands what it means to be understood. "A smart, lively play." –*NY Times.* "[A] bright and boldly provocative drama." –*Associated Press.* [3M, 2W] ISBN: 978-0-8222-2751-9

DRAMATISTS PLAY SERVICE, INC.
440 Park Avenue South, New York, NY 10016 212-683-8960 Fax 212-213-1539
postmaster@dramatists.com www.dramatists.com